Psalms, Hymns & Spiritual Songs

Making Melody to the Lord with Your Heart!

52 Devotions for Encouragement & Hope

Created & Compiled by
Dr. Randy C. Lind & Rick Boyd

Copyright ©2023 by Baptist General Convention of Oklahoma
All rights reserved
Printed in the United States of America

ISBN: 978-0-9841370-0-8

Published by Baptist General Convention of Oklahoma
3800 N. May Avenue, Oklahoma City, OK 73112

Scripture versions:

(CSB) Christian Standard Bible®, Copyright ©2017 by Holman Bible Publishers. Used by permission. Christian Standard Bible® and CSB® are federally registered trademarks of Holman Bible Publishers.

(ESV®) Bible, The Holy Bible, English Standard Version®, copyright © 2001 by Crossway, a publishing ministry of Good News Publishers. Used by permission. All rights reserved.

(ICB) International Children's Bible®. Copyright ©1986, 1988, 1999 by Thomas Nelson. Used by permission. All rights reserved.

(KJV) Public Domain

(NASB®) New American Standard Bible®, Copyright ©1960, 1971, 1977, 1995, 2020 by The Lockman Foundation. Used by permission. All rights reserved.

(NIV) New International Version®, NIV® Copyright ©1973, 1978, 1984, 2011 by Biblica, Inc.® Used by permission. All rights reserved worldwide.

(NKJV) New King James Version®. Copyright ©1982 by Thomas Nelson. Used by permission. All rights reserved.

(NLT) are taken from the Holy Bible, New Living Translation, copyright ©1996, 2004, 2015 by Tyndale House Foundation. Used by permission of Tyndale House Publishers, Carol Stream, Illinois 60188. All rights reserved.

Editor: Rick Boyd
Editorial Assistants: Patricia Farewell, Laura Gandy, Martha Hoffman and Barbara Williams

Designed by Rick Boyd, BOYDesign, boydesign.net

In October of 1988, the world was captivated at the plight of three grey whales trapped in pack ice near Point Barrow, Alaska. The effort to extricate the whales became a media sensation and a feature movie was even made about it. Volunteers used chainsaws to cut holes in the thick ice at 20-yard intervals that lead the whales out to open water. The picture of those whales, trapped in cold, dark water, coming up for air every so often on a path to freedom seems to me a picture of worship. As sinners living in a sin-cursed world, we often find ourselves trapped under the weight of the darkness of our struggles and pain. And yet the moments of worship, where we come before the presence of God, serve as "holes in the ice" where we can breathe and draw strength and perspective to continue the journey to our eventual eternal home with Christ.

Psalms, Hymns, and Spiritual Songs written by worship leaders in Oklahoma and drawing from their wisdom and experience, is an excellent resource helping its reader in the much-needed moments of worship. We must follow the example of Jesus who demonstrated the importance of private worship when He made it His regular practice to go to places of solitude to pray and worship the Father (Mark 1:35). Additionally, the Apostle Paul reminded the Ephesians of the importance of corporate worship when he instructed them to use *"psalms, hymns, and spiritual songs"* in their gatherings with one another (Ephesians 5:19). I am so grateful for this excellent book, and those who have contributed to it, which will uniquely assist Christ followers in their worship of Him.

To God be the glory!

Dr. Todd Fisher
Executive Director-Treasurer
Oklahoma Baptists

Aren't you glad that when God created all of the heavenlies, all of the earth and all creatures, that He didn't stop there? As part of God's Creation, He gave us the gift of music—a gift that connects us with each other; a gift that connects us to generations; a gift that helps us express our individual worship and feelings in ways that go deeper than we can imagine. Most of all, He gave us the gift of music so we can express our worship to our Creator.

God's people have always been a singing people. From the song of Moses found in Exodus to the song of those gathered to worship the King of Kings and Lord of Lords in Revelation, we sing! We sing when we are happy; we sing when we are sad; we sing at special gatherings, national memorials, sacred moments, festivals, sporting events; we sing when we are in love and when love is gone. Whatever the circumstance, we sing.

You and I—as Christians—have the best reason of all to sing. We sing because we have a Savior that sings over us and that is worthy of all of our praise. Scripture reminds us *"to speak to one another in psalms, hymns, and spiritual songs, singing and making music from your heart to the Lord"* (CSB).

As you read these stories of how God has spoken to each writer through song, I wonder if you will hear another voice speaking to you. Not only the voice of the writer of the devotion, but of the One who has a special message for you. Perhaps, even a song just for you. Listen carefully.

Blessings,

Dr. Randy C. Lind
Worship & Music Ministry Partner
Oklahoma Baptists

One Year of Devotions

WEEK 1	Many Will See …	Dr. Randy C. Lind
WEEK 2	It is Well	Dru Esau
WEEK 3	Keep Your Eyes on the Prize	David Baker
WEEK 4	It is No Secret	Barbara Williams
WEEK 5	Teach Me, Lord, to Wait	BJ Hall
WEEK 6	Praising My Savior All the Day Long	Wynn Anne Hook
WEEK 7	Forgotten and Neglected	James Bradford
WEEK 8	Resting in the Lord	Dr. Lee Hinson
WEEK 9	Even If …	Angela Lind
WEEK 10	This "I" Know	Jared Landreth
WEEK 11	Resting in the Goodness of God	Micah Kersh
WEEK 12	Be Reasonable	LeAnna Hall
WEEK 13	The Next Step	Chris Justice
WEEK 14	Lord of the Harvest	Mike Neff
WEEK 15	A Song in My Heart	Gina Lasater
WEEK 16	Hope in the Storm	Dakota Unruh
WEEK 17	I Love You, Lord!	Dr. Preston Collins
WEEK 18	Thy Will	Jordan Scribner

WEEK 19	The Presence of God in Worship	Aaron Robertson
WEEK 20	The Empty Cattle Barn Song	Jeremy Welborn
WEEK 21	Majesty and Glory of Your Name	Paula Fowler
WEEK 22	Are You a Channel or a Reservoir?	B. Keith Haygood
WEEK 23	God's Power	Bob Yowell
WEEK 24	Thoughts from a Beach	Mary Mills
WEEK 25	God Has Something to Say to You	Keith Butler
WEEK 26	A Lamp for My Feet	Charla Parker
WEEK 27	The Performance Trap	Brad Henderson
WEEK 28	From One Generation to Another	Mary Holt
WEEK 29	Perfect Peace	James A. Nance
WEEK 30	Sing a New Song!	Rick Boyd
WEEK 31	Still	Holly Vallandingham
WEEK 32	The Accuser	Dr. Lee Hinson
WEEK 33	Tender, Compassionate Friend	Linda Teel
WEEK 34	Star Gazing	Deanne Maynard
WEEK 35	He Sings Over Us!	Randy Holt
WEEK 36	Miss Martha with the Dance Moves	Martha Hoffman
WEEK 37	Sing That All May Know Jesus	Jeff Elkins
WEEK 38	Wait On the Lord	Martha Peck

WEEK 39	The Checklist	James Bradford
WEEK 40	Bigger Pants is Not an Option	Walter Grady
WEEK 41	Why Do I Sing?	Betty Brown
WEEK 42	The Lord is Near	BJ Hall
WEEK 43	Quiet Answers	Patricia Farewell
WEEK 44	Step by Step for Bible Study	Allen Kimberlin
WEEK 45	Breaking the Language Barrier	Brandon Chenoweth
WEEK 46	Sheltering Arms, Comforting Arms	Barbara Williams
WEEK 47	When Melody Turns Into Movement	Cody Dunbar
WEEK 48	The Vastness of His Love	Barbara Billingsley
WEEK 49	Desperately Valuable	Gary Canfield
WEEK 50	Hymn of God's Glory	Kathy Kitterman
WEEK 51	Day by Day	Laura Gandy
WEEK 52	From Generation to Generation	Dr. Randy C. Lind

Many Will See ...

*He put a new song in my mouth, a song of praise to our God.
Many will see and fear, and put their trust in the Lord.*
Psalm 40:3 (ESV)

I can give testimony to the power of music in worship. Whenever I think of this Psalm, my mind goes back to 2014 and the Singing Churchmen of Oklahoma trip to Russia where we ministered in Moscow and Sochi during the winter Olympics. In Moscow, the Singing Churchmen were engaged in concerts and helped train and encourage our Russian friends to develop their skills and lead worship in their churches. When the Singing Churchmen traveled to Sochi, we sang—literally—everywhere we went! During the trip, we sang in small groups to share our music and the Gospel. We also sang in more formal concert settings on the trip, such as churches or large outdoor venues. At each of these concerts, I was able to experience the power of the Gospel and create memories I will never forget.

As the Singing Churchmen were singing, at one point in the

concert, I would turn to the congregation to invite them to join us as we worshipped together. Occasionally, we even tried to sing in Russian with them. Isn't it wonderful that we can use music to worship without language barriers?!

Once, as we worshiped together, I saw a man begin to walk from the back of the room. He slowly walked to the front of the church, arms outstretched and palms up, as if he were receiving a gift. As he walked, I could not read the expression on his face, but he was singing. Finally, he reached the front of the church, and while we were still singing, he dropped to his knees. Following his tradition, instead of waiting for an invitation, this man—and others as well—responded to God's prompting to come and follow Jesus.

Many times, when I am singing in church, I still remember the people who followed Christ as they heard the song of praise and then joined their voice, with countless others, in the everlasting song of the redeemed. Sing on!

Lord, thank you for giving me a song of worship. Thank you for giving me the opportunity to witness Your working in my life and the lives of others as we worship You together. Amen.

Dr. Randy C. Lind
Worship & Music Ministry Partner
Oklahoma Baptists

It Will Be Okay

*And he is before all things,
and in him all things hold together.*
COLOSSIANS 1:17 (ESV)

Have you ever received unnerving news? Maybe you or a family member developed cancer. Maybe you lost your job. Maybe you lost a loved one unexpectantly. You begin to question how much more you can handle? What else can come your way? You strive to understand why the Lord is allowing these things to transpire. Life is full of news, events and situations that we must learn to navigate daily. But through all these things, one thing remains: God is still in control. He is still on His throne, and He will always be there guiding us at every twist and turn.

One of my favorite hymns is "It Is Well with My Soul." Its author, Horatio Spafford, wrote it after tragically losing his young son in the Chicago Fire of 1871 (which also ruined him financially) and then losing his daughters when their ship collided with another sea vessel on their way to England. His wife sent him a telegram: "Saved Alone …." Inspired by her words, he wrote the words to this iconic hymn while passing near where his daughters had died. Can you imagine losing everything and still saying, "It is well with my soul"?

In 2013, Kristene DiMarco re-wrote this wonderful hymn. During the chorus and bridge, she writes: *"And through it all, through it all, my eyes are on you …. So let go, my soul, and trust in Him. The waves and wind still know His name."* Creation knows Who created it. You see this as Jesus commands the waves, *"Peace! Be still!"* And they immediately cease.

When we place Christ before all things, scripture promises that He will hold all things together. That doesn't mean your situation will go away. It doesn't mean you or your family member will be cured of the disease. It *does* mean that no matter what happens, you will be okay because you have Christ. God takes care of His children and cares for them more than anything else He's created.

Father, You are sovereign and in control. Thank you for holding me together when I can't take another step. Help me to keep my focus on You and not what is going on around me. I don't want to be like Peter sinking in the water because I took my eyes off You. Amen.

Dru Esau
Singing Church Women of Oklahoma

It Is Well, Kristene DiMarco, ©2013 Bethel Music Publishing (ASCAP)

Keep Your Eyes on the Prize

I have set the Lord continually before me; because he is at my right hand, I will not be shaken.
PSALM 16:8 (ESV)

Several years ago, I was called to be a "foreign missionary" to Houston, Texas. During my time of ministry there, I was able to develop a wonderful relationship with Joe and David, ministers of music at nearby churches. We combined our adult and handbell choirs for a couple of Christmases and were looking forward to a third such celebration. Getting together monthly to rehearse, worship, fellowship and enjoy the unity we shared in Christ was such a blessing. Through music and ministry we worked toward a common goal of sharing the Christmas story with our respective congregations. And then the unimaginable happened.

David and his family were driving back to Houston after time away with extended family in their home state of Arkansas. On a rain-slick highway, outside of Texarkana, a car driving the opposite way began to hydroplane on a curve. David swerved to his right to dodge the oncoming, out-of-control car, but that action put his door directly in its path. He took the brunt of the collision, protecting his family but costing him his life.

Later, as we gathered to celebrate David and the Lord he served, we discovered that the hymn "Be Thou My Vision" had served as his life and ministry focus. I had known this hymn for a good while, but never as I recognized it on this day.

> *"Be Thou my vision O Lord of my heart;*
> *Naught be all else to me Save that Thou art.*
> *Thou my best thought by day or by night;*
> *Waking or sleeping Thy presence my light."*

We're not promised tomorrow, or the next day, or next year. May we focus on the things that are eternal and keep our eyes always on the face of our Savior.

Lord, may Your face be ever before me as I live my life to Your glory. May I realize that it's the things that last forever that need to have my primary attention. May this hymn resonate in my life for as long as You grant me breath. Amen.

David Baker
President, 2022-2023
Singing Churchmen of Oklahoma

It is No Secret

God is our refuge and strength, an ever-present help in trouble. Therefore, we will not fear though the earth gives way, and the mountains fall into the heart of the sea.
Psalm 46:1-2 (NIV)

"This is not a mild-mannered cancer that knows how to behave itself. You have an aggressive form of breast cancer, so we must fight it aggressively. That means mastectomy, chemotherapy and radiation. Even so, there is a less than 50 percent chance that you'll be alive in five years."

These are terrifying words that no woman wants to hear. The doctor explained that my cancer was an unusual type that had no known cause … and no known cure.

On the morning of the mastectomy, as we secured a spot in the hospital parking lot, a song came on the car radio with a message that I needed—right there and right then: "It is no secret what God can do. What He's done for others He'll do for you." The powerful lyrics spoke to me, saying: *"You may have longed for added strength, your courage to renew"* and *"There is no power that can conquer you while God is on your side"* as well as *"There is no night, for in His light you never walk alone."*

Those lyrics were implanted in my heart, and I relied on them throughout the two years it took to complete the brutal treatment regimen and to recover from six subsequent surgeries. My medical team often commented on my quick recovery from each procedure. One surgeon called the results "miraculous" as he confessed his initial belief that I would not survive.

God has blessed each of the 20 years of my life since then. God loves us and wants the best for us. Trust Him. Don't be afraid. He has the power. It truly is no secret what God can do. Depend on Him and watch the miracles happen.

Thank you, dear Lord, for loving us, for providing refuge in times of trouble and for allowing us to lean on Your Almighty strength when facing overwhelming adversity. Amen.

Barbara Williams
Immediate Past President
Singing ChurchWomen of Oklahoma, East

It Is No Secret (What God Can Do), Stuart Hamblen, ©1950, Duchess Music Corp

Teach Me, Lord, to Wait

But they who wait for the LORD shall renew their strength; they shall mount up with wings like eagles; they shall run and not be weary; they shall walk and not faint.
ISAIAH 40:31 (ESV)

I first heard the song at Camp Disney. The Sunday after camp, July 4, 1976, my wife was put in Hillcrest Burn Center with third degree burns over 30 percent of her body. As I sat in the waiting room of the Burn Center, the song played over and over again in my heart:

> "They that wait upon the Lord shall renew their strength.
> They shall mount up with wings as eagles.
> They shall run and not be weary.
> They shall walk and not faint.
> Teach me Lord, teach me Lord to wait."

I knew that, somehow, God was going to use this experience to His

Glory. I didn't know how. I just knew who my God was and that He would see us through this situation.

The deacons of Adair First Baptist Church and Webbers Falls First Baptist Church stood with me in the waiting room and prayed for Connie and the hospital staff who cared for her. I had resigned that morning from Adair to accept the call to Webbers Falls. God worked a mighty work in her body. The doctors were amazed with what happened. Rather than three weeks in the Critical Room and three months in the Burn Center, she was able to go home in five days! The doctors said she would need skin grafts, but that could be done as an outpatient.

However, they didn't know the Great Physician was on the case. Not only did she not have to have skin grafts, but she also has no scars. The doctor recited the events of the week in front of 25 patients and family members in the waiting room of his office. More importantly, I was able to lead the father of a child in the Burn Center to faith in Christ.

Father, help me to daily wait on You. Let me glorify Your name as I wait. Amen.

BJ Hall
Minister of Music
Tulsa, Easton Heights
Singing Churchmen of Oklahoma

Teach Me Lord to Wait, Stuart Hamblen, ©1953. Renewed 1981 Hamblen Music Company

Praising My Savior All the Day Long

Oh, let me sing to God all my life long, sing hymns to my God as long as I live! Oh, let my song please him; I'm so pleased to be singing to God.
Psalms 104:33-35 (MSG)

Music is the gift of the Lord to touch us and instill His Word and truths in our lives. Music is the rich blessing to teach children God's Word. It is proven that they retain what they sing longer than what they learn by rote. Teach them the Ten Commandments, the Lord's Prayer, the Fruit of the Spirit and to hear the voice of Jesus as He calls them.

The gift of music is that it never leaves our hearts and mind. Music reaches out to us all our lives. One day, after I had just received devastating and life-changing news, my children were praying over me, and the Spirit began to sing comfort to me:

> "O God, You are my God, and I will ever praise You.
> O God, You are my God, and I will ever praise You.
> I will seek You in the morning,
> And I will learn to walk in Your way,
> And step by step You'll lead me,
> And I will follow You all of my days."

Each day since, I have watched for His path—step by step. The Father is so faithful. Pray His Word and songs over your family and friends. They can say each day, "This is my story, this is my song, Praising my Savior all the day long."

Father, we are so grateful for Your love and provision. We offer our lives to You as an offering of praise. Thank you for music to voice our love for You. Amen.

Wynn Anne Hook
Director
Oklahoma Baptist Children's Chorus
Singing Church Women of Oklahoma

Step by Step, David (Beaker) Strasser/Michael W. Smith, ©1991 BMG Songs, Inc./Kid Brothers of St. Frank Music Publishing (ASCAP), (admin. By Brentwood-Benson Music Publishing, Inc.)

Forgotten and Neglected

The revelation of your words brings light and gives understanding to the inexperienced.
PSALM 119:130 (CSB)

A few years ago, I had a man come to me after morning worship and thank me for singing all four verses of a particular hymn. Honestly, I was a little taken aback because I thought I generally included most, if not all, of the verses of the hymns we sing. In reality, I frequently skip one of the verses (usually the third verse) because of time. Most ministers of music are held responsible for "programming" a service to be finished on time. Adding baptism, a mission's video, rambling announcements and a long-winded preacher can make folks a little nervous. After all, the cafeteria is waiting! Thus, the third verse of many hymns is often ignored. So why does the third verse get such a bad rap? I wonder if time management is the only reason. Perhaps even music ministers pay little attention to the text. But, if you take the time, you will discover many third verses are the most meaningful and compelling.

As a young boy, I was fascinated by the alto part in our hymnal. Singing along in alto, if a verse wasn't sung, I went back (usually during the sermon) and sang the missing verse in my head. As God often does, He used many "third verses" to touch my heart.

"The Old Rugged Cross" by George Bennard captured a beautiful text to make Christ's suffering on the cross seem real.

> *"In the old rugged cross, stained with blood so divine,*
> *Such a wonderful beauty I see;*
> *For 'twas on that old cross Jesus suffered and died*
> *To pardon and sanctify me."*

Dorothy Thrupp penned the powerful words of "Savior, Like A Shepherd Lead Us." Verse three literally helped me seal my salvation as an 11-year-old boy.

> *"Thou hast promised to receive us,*
> *Poor and sinful though we be;*
> *Thou hast promised to relieve us,*
> *Grace to cleanse, and pow'r to free."*

The next time you're in a worship service and the third verse is not sung, check it out. You just might find a real treasure.

Dear Lord, thank you for the revelation of Your Word. May we be strengthened and encouraged by the truth expressed in the great hymns of our faith. Amen.

James Bradford
Minister of Music
OKC, Quail Springs

Orchestra Director
Singing Churchmen of Oklahoma

Resting in the Lord

Rest in God alone, my soul, for my hope comes from him.
PSALM 62:5 (CSB)

You just need to get some rest. Take a nap. Go to bed earlier. Rest. The casual way we understand that word makes it difficult to grasp the concept of resting in God. The connotation for most of us is that resting is a rather passive thing. But the truth of Scripture is that resting in God is not passive but a purposeful positioning of ourselves within His will. It is active waiting; not a time to do nothing.

During this past year, my wife and I entered that stage in life called retirement. Now we can relax and get some rest ... or so we thought. In some physical ways, that was indeed what happened. However, it turned out to be a time of decisions, uncertainty and transition. Mental and emotional rest was harder to come by. Jesus said in Matthew 11:28-29 to come to Him and "you will find rest for your souls."

One day while leading the song "He Will Hold Me Fast" in worship, the truth came home that resting in God is worship. And worship is active, not passive. "I could never keep my hold through life's fearful path. For my love is often cold, He must hold me fast." When we respond to God's presence, power and activity in our lives, that is biblical worship. Did those decisions and uncertainties disappear? No. But Christ stood by us, carried us, worked on our behalf and provided a shelter for our spirits.

O Lord of my life, I trust in You. I pour out my heart to You and rely on the strength which comes from You. Help me to rest in Your will and take refuge in You. Amen.

Dr. Lee Hinson
Associate Pastor of Worship and Education
MWC, Sooner
Singing Churchmen of Oklahoma

He Will Hold Me Fast, ©2013 Getty Music Publishing and Matthew Merker Music, admin. by Music Services

Even If...

"If we are thrown into the blazing furnace, the God who we serve is able to save us. He will rescue us from your power, Your Majesty. But even if he doesn't, we want to make it clear to you, Your Majesty, that we will never serve your gods or worship the gold statue you have set up."

Daniel 3:17-18 (NLT)

If God is good, why do bad things happen to good people? Can we trust God? These have been the underlying questions that I have faced in the storms of life.

The song "Even If" by Mercy Me was playing on the car radio during a time when life's storms were surrounding me. My mother's health was failing, I was just told I had kidney cancer, one of my best friends passed away, and not kidding, I received a letter from the IRS informing me that I was going to be audited—all within a two-month period.

I felt I was in the path of a hurricane, and there was no place to run. Turning to the Lord and placing my trust in Him was the only decision I chose to make. Then God came and carried me through the eye of the storm, and as life's troubles seemed to swirl around me, God's hand came and covered me with His love and peace.

As Christians, we are not promised a life filled with ease, comfort, health, wealth and happiness, but we are promised God's presence in all situations. And EVEN IF the outcome is not what we pictured for our lives, we are never alone.

The God of the ages—who is not bound by time and space, who is victorious over death and the grave—knows me, knows my NAME. He has written all my days before they have happened. He is a good Father and the giver of good gifts.

"I know You're able and I know You can save through the fire with Your mighty hand But even if You don't my hope is You alone. I know the sorrow, and I know the hurt would all go away if You'd just say the word. But even if You don't my hope is You alone."

So, I choose to trust Him and His perfect will. And even if I face more storms and more trials, my hope is in Him alone.

Dear Lord, each new morning as I begin my day, I choose to surrender my life into Your hands. Lord, I trust You to guide my life and to show me Your ways. Jesus, You are all I need.

Angela Lind
President
Singing ChurchWomen of Oklahoma, West

Even If, Bart Millard/Ben Glover/Crystal Lewis/David Garcia/Tim Timmons, ©2017 Capitol Christian Music Group, Capitol CMG Publishing, Essential Music Publishing, Kobalt Music Publishing Ltd., Music Services, Inc, Spirit Music Group

This "I" Know

"As for you, you meant evil against me, but God meant it for good in order to bring about this present result …"
GENESIS 50:20 (NASB)

In January 2022, my wife had just delivered our second son. He was completely healthy, and we were so happy. A few days later, our oldest (who is 2) ended up in the hospital with breathing complications. At the time, COVID-19 was a large concern in the hospitals and only one of us was allowed to stay with him. He was on an oxygen machine for several days. My wife and I were broken—gripped with worry for our son who was struggling to breathe (for some unknown reason) and separated while she stayed with our newborn.

> *"This we know. We will see the enemy run.*
> *This we know. We will see the victory come.*
> *We hold on to every promise You ever made.*
> *Jesus, You are unfailing."*

As I sang the chorus of "This We Know" a few weeks after our oldest had recovered and returned home, I thought back to what we had gone through. At the time, it was so hard to see the "victory" in what we went through. It was hard to see God at work while my son was hooked up to an oxygen machine and my wife was home alone with our newborn. But in that moment God reminded me that my idea of "victory" is not the victory that God has planned for me.

In Genesis 50, Joseph was in a position to show revenge to his brothers who left him for dead. Instead, he told them that God had turned what they meant for evil into good. My encouragement to you is this: God is near. When you face trials, know that God is indeed fighting for you. And even though you may not see it, He has incredible plans for you. Be comforted that in your sinful and helpless estate, Christ saved you and you have an eternity with Him to look towards.

God, thank you that You are the one who is in control. Help me know that what You have for me is far greater than anything I could plan for myself. Help me trust You and be obedient in following You today. Amen.

Jared Landreth
Creative Arts & Worship Minister
Shawnee, Immanuel
Oklahoma Worship Collective

This We Know, Jason Ingram/Kristian Stanfill, ©2016 Open Hands Music, So Essential Tunes

Resting in the Goodness of God

*But when I thought how to understand this,
it seemed to me a wearisome task, until I went into
the sanctuary of God; then I discerned their end.*
PSALM 73:16-17 (ESV)

Several years ago, I did a study of the Psalms of Asaph. Asaph was a Levite appointed by King David for the leading of songs before the Ark of the covenant. He was the writer of 12 Psalms—Psalm 73-83 as well as Psalm 50. You see in his writing a man who loved God deeply and had seen the Lord do amazing things. However, He is also very aware of the depravity and brokenness of the world.

In Psalm 73, Asaph begins by declaring God is good. He wants to drive that truth home because what he continues to write seems to be a crisis of faith. Asaph is greatly concerned and distressed over what seems to be the blessing of the wicked. All around him he sees wickedness and brokenness. And he struggles with the question of how could those who are rebelling against God seem to be receiving the blessing of health and riches. He knows God is good but is questioning how God is showing his goodness.

Then in verse 16 and 17 there is a turning point for Asaph. He says, *"But when I thought how to understand this, it seemed to me a wearisome task, until I went into the sanctuary of God; then I discerned their end."* When Asaph entered the presence and the glory of God his perspective changed from what is temporary to what is eternal. As followers of Jesus, how do we define what is good? Asaph gives us the answer at the end of this Psalm when he says, *"But for me it is good to be near God."*

The first time this Psalm really impacted my life was at a conference several years ago when we were given one hour of solitude and prayer. I read this Psalm, and the Lord used it to show me His perspective and helped me to see His goodness in my life. In fact, it provoked me to write a song called "No one Else." The song simply proclaims that no one knows me like God. Only God knows the dark, secret places of my soul. Though that is true, it is also true that no one *loves* me like God. I can rest in that truth.

God, I thank You. Give me eyes to see as You see and help me to rest in Your goodness. Amen.

Micah Kersh
Worship Pastor
Newcastle, First
Oklahoma Worship Collective

Be Reasonable

Come now, let us reason together, says the Lord: though your sins are like scarlet, they shall be as white as snow; though they are red like crimson, they shall become like wool.
ISAIAH 1:18 (ESV)

The Lord invites His people to come reason with Him. God's direction for us is reasonable. It is smart! It is the best way to live. It would be madness to reject and resist a God of infinite wisdom, infinite love, infinite grace and infinite power. True reason will drive an honest man to humble adoration and submission to God. It is just plain reasonable to follow God.

Have you ever heard of a Christian, on his deathbed, with family and friends gathered around, say: "Watch out for that Christianity! I've followed Jesus my whole life and I regret it! What a waste of time! What nonsense!" I hardly think so. Quite the opposite, we find Christians on their deathbed trusting in God more than ever! That is what is reasonable!

There is tremendous hope in God's forgiveness! We really can be clean from the stain of sin. Our good works don't clean the stain, and death can't clean the stain—only the work of Jesus can make us white as snow. The power of sin, the shame of sin, the guilt of sin, the domination of sin, the terror of sin and the pain of sin are all taken away in Jesus. Isaiah doesn't mention how this cleansing comes, but we who live on the other side of the Cross know that it comes because Jesus took upon Himself our stain of sin. Jesus bore God's judgment of our sin, so we can be as white as snow and as white as wool. Come now … let us reason together.

Lord, thank you for paying the penalty for my sin. Thank you for shedding your crimson blood to turn my scarlet sin as white as snow. Amen.

LeAnna Hall
Singing Church Women of Oklahoma

The Next Step

For we walk by faith, not by sight.
2 Corinthians 5:7 (CSB)

We've all experienced those dreaded power outages, in the late evening, when we cannot see a thing. We slowly make our way through the house looking for the flashlight, all while trying not to step on a LEGO® or stub our toe on the dresser. Once we find the flashlight, assuming the batteries are not dead, we turn it on. Now we can see what is in front of us. Our next step is lit up.

Our journey with the Lord can be a lot like that as well. Wouldn't it be nice if God kept all the lights on all the time so we could see where we're going? But most of the time, God gives us just enough light for us to trust Him to lead us.

I can remember many times in my ministry, and in my walk with Christ, when God showed me very clearly every step to take. I can also think of many times when I struggled to know what step to take or even if there was another step.

The first time I heard the song "Bow the Knee" was many years ago when Chris Machen, one of the writers of the song, came and led a choir retreat for us. I did not need it at that moment, but God knew there would be times when I would need a reminder to trust Him. I'm sure you've needed that reminder as well. Let me encourage you, just as the song says, to "trust the heart of the Father" and "believe the One who holds eternity." He will guide you even when you cannot see the path.

Lord, guide me every step of my journey. I want to remain on Your path even when I cannot see the next step. Amen.

Chris Justice
Worship Pastor
Moore, Regency Park

Principal Pianist/Tenor 2 Section Leader
Singing Churchmen of Oklahoma

Bow the Knee, Mike Harland and Chris Machen, ©1997 Centergetic Music (ASCAP) (admin. by ICG)

Lord of the Harvest

Then he said to his disciples, "The harvest is abundant, but the workers are few. Therefore, pray to the Lord of the harvest to send out workers into his harvest."
MATTHEW 9:37-38 (CSB)

I'm a "farm boy" at heart! I know this sounds weird, but I love the smell of freshly plowed soil. Truly, there is nothing like breathing in the fresh air and the richness of the earth's soil. It is organic, full of minerals and the perfect mix of sand, silt, clay and decay. Good soil is a must to grow a good crop.

Growing a crop takes months of preparation! I learned to appreciate all aspects of farming because my dad is a good farmer. He has been farming my entire adult life. There is a lot of hard work that goes into farming before a crop is produced. Two of the most important items in farming are the seed and the soil. Good seed usually produces a good crop, but that seed first needs to be planted in fertile soil. The sower of the seed must scatter the seed before it will grow. But weather can make or break a crop! Whether a farmer acknowledges it or not, reliance on God to send rain at the right times—without damaging winds or hail so the crop grows and is ready for harvest—takes faith and trust in Sovereign God.

As a child, our music and youth minister sang the Imperials song "Lord of the Harvest" for the offertory one Sunday.

> "See the fields ripe and white as snow. Up from the seeds of faith we planted long ago. So many the hearts in season, with every prayer they've grown. He has made them ready, but we must bring them home."

> "Lord of the harvest place Your fire in me. Servants You need now; your Servant I will be. Give me the eyes of Your Spirit, Your heart of compassion to know. Lord of the harvest show me where to go."

The words of the song still impact my ministry today.

God, only You know the lasting impact of seed scattered on the soil of my ministry. I pray the Gospel impact is everlasting as the Holy Spirit brings many to the truth of salvation. May I continue to humbly prepare the fields for the Lord of the harvest! Amen.

Mike Neff
Administrator
Lawton, First

Former President
Singing Churchmen of Oklahoma

Lord of the Harvest, words by Paul Smith, music by James Newton Howard, ©1982 Marquis Iii Music, Newton House Music, Word Music LLC, Dayspring Music LLC

A Song in My Heart

I will be glad and exult in you; I will sing praise to your name, O Most High.
PSALM 9:2 (ESV)

Have you ever had something happen in your life that seemed to steal your joy? Several years ago my son chose an alternate lifestyle that broke my heart. I felt like I would never be able to sing again.

However, God reminded me through His Word that my joy is in Him. I immediately began singing:

> "There's within my heart a melody,
> Jesus whispers sweet and low.
> Fear not I am with thee peace, be still,
> in all of life's ebb and flow."

These words are still such a comfort to me. His song is always in my heart for He keeps me singing.

Dear Lord, thank you for keeping Your song in my heart and for reminding me that my joy is always found in You. Amen.

Gina Lasater
Historian, 2021-2022
Singing Church Women of Oklahoma

Hope in the Storm

Why are you cast down, O my soul, and why are you in turmoil within me? Hope in God; for I shall again praise him, my salvation and my God.
Psalm 42:5-6a (ESV)

It was my first year in full-time ministry, and it was off to a great start—then the COVID-19 pandemic swept through the country. Everything shut down, and many challenges arose in my life and ministry. I found myself going through issues I would never have imagined, as I'm sure you faced as well.

It was during this time I began to feel alone. Living on my own and not meeting regularly with the church caused loneliness to creep in. Also during this time, I was burdened with the loss of so many lives in our church and across the country. Then my sister received a medical diagnosis we did not expect or desire to hear. It was during these trials the Lord reminded me to look to Him through the lyrics of "Lord from Sorrows Deep I Call."

"O my soul, put your hope in God.
My help, my rock, I will praise Him.
Sing, O sing, through the raging storm.
You're still my God, my salvation."

I was reminded God is in control in the storm. He is unchanging and gives us hope through salvation by Jesus Christ. I was also reminded to praise Him at all times, not just when things are going well. In the midst of turmoil, I could praise God, placing my hope in Him.

God, when the storms rage and all seems hopeless, You are still God and in control. Help me to praise You in the storm and thank You for the hope found in salvation through Jesus Christ. Amen.

Dakota Unruh
Minister of Music/Associate Pastor
Durant, Calvary
Singing Churchmen of Oklahoma

Lord from Sorrows Deep I Call, Matt Papa/Matt Boswell, ©2018 Getty Music Hymns and Songs (Admin. by Music Services, Inc.), Getty Music Publishing (Admin. by Music Services, Inc.), Love Your Enemies Publishing (Admin. by Music Services, Inc.), Messenger Hymns (Admin. by Music Services, Inc.)

I Love You, Lord!

He is the image of the invisible God, the firstborn of all creation. For by him all things were created, in heaven and on earth, visible and invisible, whether thrones or dominions or rulers or authorities—all things were created through him and for him. And he is before all things, and in him all things hold together. And he is the head of the body, the church. He is the beginning, the firstborn from the dead, that in everything he might be preeminent. For in him all the fullness of God was pleased to dwell, and through him to reconcile to himself all things, whether on earth or in heaven, making peace by the blood of his cross.
Colossians 1:15-20 (ESV)

Before we were married, Jan and I were best friends. After more than 45 years of marriage and ministry, we're still best friends. When you know someone better, you can love them more.

The youth group was singing a new and simple worship song that basically said, "I love You, Lord," over and over again. I'm so glad we're teaching young people to express their love for God, and we all need to know the One we love.

A hymn from the 60s can help us know Him better. Not written in the "1960s" or "1860s" or even the "1760s." This hymn was written by a missionary while imprisoned for preaching Jesus in the AD 60s. From a Roman prison, Paul wrote to encourage the Colossians to know Jesus better and walk in Him. In the hymn above, we see that Jesus is Lord over all creation, including that which we observe through a telescope or a microscope. He is also Lord of the invisible parts of creation. Without Jesus, all creation would not exist. Today, Jesus is holding creation together. We live under the law of gravity, but the law of gravity is under His control.

Jesus is Lord over the church. If you want to be head of a church, just raise yourself from the dead. Until then, Jesus *alone* is Lord of the church. We are called to serve under His authority, following His direction, in His church.

Jesus is Lord of reconciliation. By the Cross, we are reconciled to Holy God. By faith, we receive Jesus as Lord. And by words and actions, we express thanksgiving to our God who saved us.

Jesus, today let my words and my actions proclaim to all people that You alone are my Lord. I love You, Lord! Amen.

Dr. Preston Collins
Executive Director
Union Baptist Association
Oklahoma Baptist Symphony

Thy Will

Our Father which art in heaven, Hallowed be Thy name. Thy kingdom come. Thy will be done in earth, as it is in heaven.
MATTHEW 6:9-10 (KJV)

In the spring of 2016, I was laid off from a job that I loved. While the layoff was based solely on budgetary constraints, I still felt hurt, betrayed and confused. In my devastation, I couldn't see how God was working in me and through me.

That same spring, Hillary Scott released her Grammy-winning single "Thy Will." When I heard the song, I found myself in tears, crying out to the Lord with the lyrics: *"I may never understand that my broken heart is a part of your plan"* and *"when I try to pray, all I've got is hurt and these four words: Thy will be done."*

While the song initially served as a catharsis for me, God used the song to transform me, and through me, He began to change the hearts of those around me.

One day, from the most unlikely person, I received a note detailing a re-dedication of faith in Jesus Christ. It said, "Your grace and unselfishness during these times are a testament that you walk with God. This has been a time of prayer and reflection for me, and I'm going to turn my life over to Him."

How amazing is it that God used one of my greatest disappointments in life to lead someone to the greatest blessing in their life—a relationship with our Savior, Jesus Christ!

Thank you, Father, that You see me and hear me in my time of need. When my path is dark, help me to trust and follow You faithfully. Thank you, Lord, for Your plans to prosper me and the goodness You have in store. Thy will be done! Amen.

Jordan Scribner
The Singing Church Women, West

Thy Will, Bernie Herms/Hillary Dawn Scott/Emily Weisband, ©2016 EKT Publishing, WB Music Corp., Thankful for This Music, and Co-Publisher

The Presence of God in Worship

*When the song was raised ... in praise to the L*ORD *...*
*the house of the L*ORD, *was filled with a cloud, so that the*
priests could not stand to minister because of the cloud,
*for the glory of the L*ORD *filled the house of God.*
2 CHRONICLES 5:13-14 (ESV)

Have you ever had an encounter with God that was so strong you could feel His presence? I can count on my hands the number of times I've experienced the life-changing, manifest presence of God in worship. The first time it happened I was at a concert where the artists took time in the middle of their set to spend time in pure praise to God. Another time was the first time I attended a service at the Brooklyn Tabernacle in New York.

It's not that I don't believe Christ's presence is with me all the time—I do. But there is something special that happens when the people of God come together and praise the Lord with one voice.

His presence falls in a mighty way. And the few times He has manifested Himself this way leave me longing for everyone I know to experience the joy His presence brings in worship.

Father, thank you for your presence in our lives through the indwelling of your Spirit. As we gather for worship this week, may Your people praise you with one voice, and may Your presence fall in a powerful and life-changing way.

Aaron Robertson
Minister of Worship & Media
Ponca City, First
Singing Churchmen of Oklahoma

The Empty Cattle Barn Song

Even though the fig trees have no blossoms, and there are no grapes on the vines; ... even though the flocks die in the fields, and the cattle barns are empty, yet I will rejoice in the Lord! I will be joyful in the God of my salvation!
HABAKKUK 3:17-18 (NLT)

This particular passage of hope in the midst of despair is one that I memorized as a teenager. It has served as a reminder to rejoice in the Lord through several particularly dark times in my life and continues to serve me well today as I navigate what is arguably the most difficult period of despair that I have ever experienced.

In Habakkuk's day, the world looked incredibly bleak when the crops failed and livestock was in short supply. Yet even in the middle of an empty cattle barn, Habakkuk was able to sing a song of joy to the Lord. And it wasn't at the point when God came through by miraculously filling the cattle barn that Habakkuk sang a song of joy, but rather when all hope was lost. All except the hope that Habakkuk had in the Lord God Almighty.

I, too, find great strength when I sing songs of joy to the God of my salvation, even when salvation has yet to arrive. Just knowing that He is the God of my salvation is enough to cause me to sing the "empty cattle barn" song. I hope you will sing it with me too!

Father, today I will rejoice in You, for You are the God of my salvation! Amen.

Jeremy Welborn
Former President
Singing Churchmen of Oklahoma

Majesty and Glory of Your Name

> *O Lord, our Lord, how majestic is your name in all the earth! You have set your glory above the heavens. From the lips of children and infants you have ordained praise …*
> PSALM 8:1-2A (NIV)

What really grabs your attention? Have you ever just stood and admired the mountains, sky, ocean? God's beauty and majesty can be seen everywhere you turn. Have you been on a trip to the mountains, driven through the badlands, looked down the Grand Canyon? As a kid our vacations consisted of going to these places. The awesomeness of being in the mountains of Colorado and gazing into a clear, blue, icy-cold lake can leave one speechless.

There is a song, "Majesty and Glory," that describes the awesomeness, the majesty and glory of who God is. In Psalm 8, King David did his best to convey that even the name of God is majestic, not only in heaven but on earth as well. "Majesty and

Glory" is a song that reaches to my very soul. It is hard for me to sing or listen to this song without tears. Do you have a song that causes you to pause and ponder the words you are reading or singing?

For several years I have led the Wacky Science activity at Camp Perfect Wings at CrossTimbers Camp in Davis, Oklahoma. One of the activities is for campers to discover that no two fingerprints are alike. They ink their thumb and press it to a card, then look at their own fingerprint and compare their print with someone else's. No two prints are alike.

Think of all the people who have been born and will be born up until the last person before the Rapture. No two fingerprints will be alike. This fact speaks volumes about the awesomeness of God. David spent much time alone with God in praise, presenting his heartaches, asking for forgiveness and guidance, acknowledging who God is and proclaiming God's majesty and glory. How much time do you spend each day talking to God and pondering His majesty and glory?

Father in heaven, how majestic is Your name above all others. Thank you for your creation. Help me to never lack in my praise and worship of You or neglect to stand in awe of Your marvelous works. May I always remember to give You thanks. Amen.

Paula Fowler
Singing ChurchWomen of Oklahoma

Are You a Channel or a Reservoir?

> *In Christ, God was reconciling the world to himself, not counting their trespasses against them, and entrusting to us the message of reconciliation. ... We implore you on behalf of Christ, be reconciled to God. For our sake he made him to be sin who knew no sin, so that in him we might become the righteousness of God.*
> 2 CORINTHIANS 5:19-21 (ESV)

I love to go to the mountains. Driving through the mountains, the roads typically follow a rushing river. In the summer, the snow melting on the tops of the mountains feeds the rivers with a roaring rush of water. I love it when I drive into a valley and see a reservoir that is fed by those rushing waters. Typically, these reservoirs are quiet, serene and peaceful. When compared to the rolling waters of the river, it is a place where the water has come to rest.

I often think about the comparison of the river and the reservoir.

Many of us have been programmed to work hard for many years in preparation for retirement. And I look forward to that someday myself. But, my friends, I think we need to be reminded that life happens in the rushing river.

When we are busy serving the Lord, there is activity, there is movement, there is work. When we stop serving the Lord and focus completely on the serenity of the reservoir, we lose sight of the work still to be done. Most of us raised in church will remember the old gospel hymn "Make Me A Channel of Blessing."

"Is your life a channel of blessing? Is the love of God flowing through you? Are you telling the lost of the Savior? Are you ready, His service to do? Make me a channel of blessing today, Make me a channel of blessing, I pray, My life possessing, my service blessing, make me a channel of blessing today."

There is nothing wrong with retirement from our work. But when we do retire, our service to God should continue (and perhaps, even grow). In serving the Lord, don't look forward to the quiet of the reservoir. Stay in the river, where life happens and where you can make a difference in the lives of others.

Thank you, God, for the blessing of men and women who have invested in my life and have been a channel of blessing for me. Help me to allow You to reproduce in others what You have done in my life. Make me a channel of blessing. Put me in the current of the Holy Spirit's work. Amen.

B. Keith Haygood
Executive Pastor of Fine Arts
Edmond, First

Jazz Band Director
Singing Churchmen of Oklahoma

God's Power

*But he said to me, "My grace is sufficient for you,
for my power is made perfect in weakness."*
2 CORINTHIANS 12:9 (NIV)

*He gives strength to the weary and
increases the power of the weak.*
ISAIAH 40:29 (NIV)

I was recovering from what would become my most painful surgery ever. These were already "dark" days for my wife and me, and it seemed they might get worse. "We" had cancer. Day one passed, and then came days two and three. The anesthesia wore off, pain took over and I was literally begging for something for the pain. Finally, the nurse brought the miracle IV. She explained how this IV thing would help alleviate my pain. Whenever I hurt, I should push the button and I get a dose of "pain med." There was power in that button. Button and I became close friends.

God began to speak spiritual truths as I lay there, and I remembered the words to the hymn "There Is Power In The Blood." There was power in that button, and I realized God's power is so available to us. God's power for so many things is always there to lean on. Instead of just pushing the button, I was praying "God, it hurts so bad, in Jesus' name, please I need relief." He added His power. We don't have to plug in to a wall socket; no need for an AC/DC adapter; don't even have to be in a hospital.

One afternoon my wife was standing by my bed, and she knew I was hurting. I pushed the button. Relief! Then she noticed a small puddle spreading beneath my bed. The tube had disconnected from my arm. The pain med was spilling on the floor. I don't know how long I had been pushing the button and was still getting relief! When earthly things failed, God provided the relief I needed. Yes, I believed in the button, but it was faith in God, faith in the Power of God that worked.

God, thank you that Your amazing, incredible power is real and is available in any situation, anytime, anywhere. Power to forgive sin. Power to save. Even the power to calm pain in a hospital bed or anywhere people need Your touch. Amen.

Bob Yowell
Co-leader, Bass Section
Singing Churchman of Oklahoma
Royce Brown Award Recipient

Thoughts from a Beach

*Carefully consider the path for your feet, and
all your ways will be established. Don't turn to
the right or to the left; keep your feet away from evil.*
Proverbs 4:26-27 (CSB)

On a recent trip to Florida, I was looking forward to the time I would spend on a beautiful, pristine beach. To my dismay, upon arrival, I discovered the entire beach was covered in a blanket of seaweed that had washed ashore. As I walked toward the ocean, I found that the seaweed did not feel good to my bare feet. But since it was everywhere, there seemed no escape. Looking closer, I saw small patches of sand intermingled with the seaweed. I realized that if I stepped onto these patches, my feet would have been protected from the abrasive seaweed. However, to do that, I had to keep my eyes focused on this protective pathway of sand "islands."

That got me thinking about my walk with the Lord. Sometimes

I veer off track, into painful territory, because I'm not keeping my eyes focused on the One who deserves my attention—the only One who has the power to save. As I carefully walked across the beach, a hymn came to mind.

> *"Turn your eyes upon Jesus,*
> *Look full in His wonderful face,*
> *And the things of earth will grow strangely dim,*
> *In the light of His glory and grace."*

Its message is as true today as it was when it was penned 100 years ago.

Jesus, thank you for being my Savior! Keep me focused on Your ways. Help me to follow Your path every day. Amen.

Mary Mills
Singing Church Women of Oklahoma

God Has Something to Say to You

Make me to know your ways, O Lord; teach me your paths. Lead me in your truth and teach me, for you are the God of my salvation; for you I wait all the day long.
PSALM 25:4-5 (ESV)

I was at Falls Creek encampment following my senior year of high school, and we were having the final devotion time at our cabin. Facing the future, I shared my uncertainty about what God would have me do with my life. I loved music and sort of expected God to call me to be a Minister of Music while at Falls Creek. I thought it might happen during the B.B. McKinney hymn—whose hymn tune is Falls Creek—"Wherever He Leads I'll Go."

Well, the very first invitation hymn that week was "Wherever He Leads I'll Go." I waited for the Holy Spirit to speak and give me direction. It didn't come. I was pretty devastated. I was ready, but it seemed my plan wasn't God's plan. The last public invitation of the week was on Saturday morning. "My Jesus, I Love Thee" was the song. It was the first and the last time I heard that hymn used as an invitation. While singing the first words of the first verse, I felt God speaking to me like He had never spoken before. The Spirit of the Lord overflowed my heart, and I was at the front of the tabernacle before I knew it. I was privileged to serve as a Minister of Music for more than 50 years.

I'm reminded of a chorus written by "Uncle Gene Bartlett." The words went: "God has something to say to you, God has something to say. Listen, listen, pay close attention, God has something to say." My problem was I was not listening to God. I was too busy trying to determine how, when and where the Lord was directing me. I wasn't paying attention to His voice.

Certainly, I did not plan to get drafted from the seminary into the Army. That, however, was the Lord's path for me. I grew spiritually, and even musically, as I was privileged to direct a children's choir and a youth choir while in the army. Also, while serving, our first child was born with difficulties that required immediate surgery. God's hand was on us with remarkable medical care and a 19-day hospital stay that cost only $25.

Lord, help me to listen and obey, confident that Your way is always the right way, even when I don't understand why. Thank you for being the God of my salvation and for sending Your Son to die on the cross to give me everlasting life. Amen.

Keith Butler
Minister of Music, Retired
Singing Churchmen of Oklahoma
Royce Brown Award Recipient

A Lamp for My Feet

Thy Word is a lamp for my feet and a light on my path.
PSALM 119:105 (CSB)

The first time I heard the song "Thy Word" by Amy Grant and Michael W. Smith was at Glorieta Conference Center during Music Week. I have always loved this verse from the Scripture, and I immediately felt a strong kinship to the song. I especially love the words of the second verse:

> *"I will not forget,*
> *Your love for me and yet,*
> *My heart forever is wandering.*
> *Jesus, be my guide."*

In my Christian walk with God, I always need to look to Him daily—and hourly—for guidance and the willingness to follow Him as my guide. He has led me and kept me and loved me for all these years ... and continues to do so. When I forget to seek Him and follow Him is when this *"lamp for my feet and light on my path"* becomes even more real and needed. I pray that God will continue to lead me in the path He would have me go.

Dear Lord, please lead me daily with Your lamp and Your light. I cannot live without them or without You as my guide. I love You and will love You to the end. Amen.

Charla Parker
Singing ChurchWomen of Oklahoma

Thy Word, Amy Grant/Michael W. Smith, ©1984 Word Music, LLC/Meadowgreen Music Company (admin. by EMI CMG publishing)

The Performance Trap

*And may you have the power to understand,
as all God's people should, how wide, how long,
how high, and how deep his love is.*
EPHESIANS 3:18 (NLT)

Years ago, I taught in the university setting and one of my favorite assignments was leading a student jazz group. One of the students was a young lady named Tiffany. Tiff is one of the most gifted singers I've ever heard. She could sing a convincing aria, get down ala Whitney Houston and her jazz stylings were spot on. She slept, ate and lived in the world of musical performance. After graduation, Tiff moved to Texas to work on her Masters, I began serving at FBC Tulsa and we lost touch.

Recently, Tiff reached out. While in Texas, she had met and married a fellow student named John and moved to Alabama. Now she needed my musical services at her community college teaching post. Tiff picked me up at the Birmingham Airport, and on the trip back to college, we had lunch at a local diner. As a conversation starter, I asked about her husband and how they met.

Remember, this is a young lady whose entire life, and much of her self-worth, was tied up in how well she performed—a common scenario among artists. As she began their story, Tiff said she and John had met in grad school, he in seminary and she in vocal performance studies. Her words were: "I remember thinking there's something very special about this guy." Then one of the most significant things I've ever heard spoken by another human being followed. "And Brad, (she started to cry) he told me he loved me before he ever heard me sing."

We both sat there, stunned at the significance of her statement. That moment of crystal-clear truth will be always in the front of my mind. The honest truth is that's EXACTLY how God loves us. His love is pure, absolutely not based on our performance.

Perhaps you've seen the refrigerator magnet that states: "Yes, Jesus loves me ... but He loves me MORE when I sing." What an absolute lie! God loves you BEFORE He hears you sing. Be amazed by this profound truth.

Lord, help me understand the width and height and depth of Your love for me. May I never forget that Your great love is extravagant, amazing, unstoppable and unconditional. Amen.

Brad Henderson
Worship Associate
Tulsa, First
Director
Oklahoma Baptist Symphony

From One Generation to Another

*One generation shall praise Your works to another,
And shall declare Your mighty acts.*
PSALM 145:4 (NASB)

As a young piano student, I had Stanley Miles as my Minister of Music. He saw a 9-year-old girl trying to learn a new hymn every week and asked her to play with a seasoned organist during Wednesday evening prayer services. It was just one hymn each week, but he invested time with me prior to each service to make sure my chords and timing were correct. That year of Wednesday nights led to me playing in handbell choirs and accompanying youth choirs.

Those hymns I learned became the foundation of my love for Christ and His church. The words of "At Calvary," "Tell Me the Story of Jesus" and "Sweet Hour of Prayer" are written on my heart as deeply as the words of Mark 12:30: *"Love the Lord your God with all your heart, mind, soul and strength."*

Israel Houghton, in his song "You Are Good," calls us to remember God's goodness and worship Him from "generation to generation."

> *"From generation to generation,*
> *we worship You.*
> *Hallelujah, Hallelujah,*
> *we worship You for who You are.*
> *You are good!"*

Through our worship, we praise God's works and declare His mighty acts. The saving love of Christ is passed from generation to generation. What impact are you having on this generation and the next?

Lord, please help me to see those of Your children who need encouragement and confidence to play, sing Your Word and share Your love with generation after generation. Amen,

Mary Holt
Pianist
Oklahoma Student Worship Choir

You Are Good, Israel Houghton, ©2001 Integrity Praise Music, Sound of the New Breed

Perfect Peace

*"My sheep hear My voice and I know them …
I give them eternal life and they shall never perish;
neither shall anyone snatch them out of My hand."*
JOHN 10:27-28 (NKJV)

*I will both lie down in peace and sleep; for You alone, O
LORD, make me dwell in safety.*
PSALM 4:8 (NKJV)

In 1971, as a 24-year-old U.S. Army lieutenant, I was sent to Vietnam to serve with the 101st Airborne Division. It was my first time to be away from family and friends for an extended time. I was scared, alone and had left my new wife of six months.

Fighting and rocket (mortar) attacks were frequent. There was no such thing as "front lines." We were assigned to a compound within a fortified perimeter. Many nights we were overrun by the

Vietcong. We often discovered evidence each morning that they had infiltrated our area during the night. I had many sleepless, restless nights and was afraid I would never make it home. I was a believer and read my Bible every chance I got, but I really had no peace about being there and wondered if God had deserted me.

Then someone showed me a hymn I had never heard before. The first stanza begins "Like a river glorious is God's perfect peace …," but it was the second stanza that began to give me hope:

> *"Hidden in the hollow of His blessed hand,*
> *Never foe can follow, never traitor stand.*
> *Not a surge of worry, not a shade of care,*
> *Not a blast of hurry touch the spirit there.*
> *Stayed upon Jehovah, hearts are fully blest;*
> *Finding, as He promised, perfect peace and rest."*

I came to realize that God would keep me safe in the "hollow of His hand." He gave me not only His perfect peace, but also hope to trust Him during the Vietnam war. I safely came home in 1972. My wife and I moved to Texas to begin my ministry training at Southwestern Seminary, and I've served the Lord more than 50 years through music ministry in Texas, Alabama and Oklahoma.

Lord, thank you for teaching me to trust You. Help me find Your perfect peace regardless of the challenges I'm facing right now. Amen.

James A. Nance
Tenor 1 Section Leader
Singing Churchmen of Oklahoma

Sing a New Song!

Oh sing to the Lord a new song; sing to the Lord, all the earth! Sing to the Lord, bless his name; tell of his salvation from day to day. Declare his glory among the nations, his marvelous works among all the peoples!
Psalm 96:1-3 (ESV)

I love the old hymns! I'm old enough to remember when that was all that was sung at church. Then, in the 1970s, a few Gaither tunes snuck into the mix. Now, it seems I'm learning a new song every week. And that's great! As special as the old hymns are, we need to remember they were once "new songs."

The Bible has a lot to say about singing new songs. In Psalm 144, David says, *"I will sing a new song to you, O God,"* and then proclaims it's such a good song, he's going to accompany himself on a ten-string harp. In Psalm 40, David declares that he can't stop himself from singing since the Lord has *"put a new song in my mouth, a song of praise to our God."* As a result, *"Many will see and fear, and put their trust in the Lord."* David felt this way because God had just delivered him *"from the pit of destruction."*

Even Isaiah, who may not have been able to carry a tune in a bucket, commands all the earth's inhabitants to *"sing to the Lord a new song"* (Isa. 42:10). And some glorious day, believers will gather in heaven where we'll be *"singing a new song before the throne"* (Rev. 14:3).

So, let's not neglect the old songs. Their messages are just as relevant and uplifting today as they were a hundred or more years ago. But let's keep writing, learning and singing new songs of praise and proclamation. New songs will always be appropriate for new rescues, fresh expressions of God's grace and the continuing proclamation of the Gospel. As long as God is gracious toward us, keeps showing us His power and dazzling us with His marvelous works, it's proper that we not just sing old songs inspired by His past grace, but that we also sing new songs about His unending grace.

Lord, put a new song in my heart! May I use it to praise Your name, strengthen my faith and declare Your marvelous works to all people. Amen.

Rick Boyd
Singing Churchmen of Oklahoma

Still

"*But the hour is coming, and is now here, when the true worshipers will worship the Father in spirit and truth, for the Father is seeking such people to worship him. God is spirit, and those who worship him must worship in spirit and truth.*"
JOHN 4:23-24 (ESV)

Even if ... but God ... still. Have you ever been there? A father of three dies suddenly after a long battle with illness right when he was thought to be on the road to recovery. A teenager's life changes forever because of a car wreck. A house burns down and everything is lost. We were never promised an easy path in this world. Yet, we were created to worship God ... even if ... still.

"*Broken, needy, You know my heart*
Tired, wounded, torn apart
Shattered longings I place in Your hand
Kneeling, unable to stand."

The year the Singing ChurchWomen were introduced to the song "Still" was shortly after my family walked through a very difficult, life-changing time in our ministry. My dad, a pastor who had faithfully led his flock for more than 18 years, was asked by the church to resign for unspecified reasons. God used the lyrics to this song to sooth my soul and help me get back to what I was meant to do: *"Still I will trust You, still I will sing, songs of thanksgiving, to my King."*

We were created to worship God and that should be our focus—day in and out, in good times and bad. Sometimes, as worship leaders, it's hard to remember why we do what we do when the path becomes dark and lonely.

That day, the natural choice would have been to turn our backs on the church and God, and to walk away, out of ministry. But that isn't our purpose in life. It's like telling a duck not to swim or a bird not to fly. God used this song to bring my focus back to where it needed to be—on Him; back to where my hope and trust needed to be—in Him and not in man. So today, years later, "my eyes are failing, Your promise fulfill, and till then, I'll worship You still."

Father, help me to always remain faithful and true to follow and worship You. Thank You for Your guidance in storms and for never giving up on me. Amen.

Holly Vallandingham
Pianist
Singing ChurchWomen of Oklahoma, East

Still, Craig Curry, ©2005 GlorySound

The Accuser

If we confess our sins, He is faithful and just to forgive us our sins and to cleanse us from all unrighteousness.
1 JOHN 1:9 (KJV)

As believers, we still struggle with sins, some greater, some smaller—but all of them in need of help from the shed blood of Christ and the merciful forgiveness of God. Sometimes, Satan, the accuser, hits me over the head with my guilt from my sin. He tells me that because I have sinned, I am not worthy to read God's word or to pray to Him. Just look at what you have done and who you are. You are guilty!

In one of those moments of spiritual battle, the lyrics from the song "Before the Throne of God Above" came to my mind: *"When Satan tempts me to despair and tells me of the guilt within."* It is a club that the old accuser has used against me all too often.

However, lest we despair, the song continues: *"Upward I look and see Him there who made an end of all my sins."* The work of Christ on the cross has handled our sin. *"For God the just is satisfied to look on Him and pardon me."*

The time when we are in the most despair over our sin is the very time to call on the Lord, seek His face and soak in His Word. We must not allow the voice of Satan to keep us from the joy of forgiveness and sweetness of fellowship with our Savior and Redeemer.

Lord Jesus, I confess my sins to You. Thank you for making an end of them and filling me with Your peace. Amen.

Dr. Lee Hinson
Associate Pastor of Worship and Education
MWC, Sooner
Singing Churchmen of Oklahoma

Before the Throne of God Above, ©1997 Sovereign Grace Worship, admin. By Integrity's Hosanna! Music

Tender, Compassionate Friend

Because of the Lord's great love, we are not consumed, for his compassions never fail. They are new every morning; great is your faithfulness.
LAMENTATIONS 3:22-23 (NIV)

My love for music started as a child and never left me. It has looked different throughout the years. As I grew in my walk with the Lord, I was more keenly aware of what was in the songs I listened to. I remember shopping with my teenage daughter one day and singing along with 70's music on the radio. She asked me how I knew the words to these songs. I told her they were "oldies." After that, I started noticing the words and messages in those songs. They were not all wholesome! It caused me to consider what message I was subconsciously learning and sending out. It really mattered to me!

I grew up singing the old hymns. Looking back, I realize what an impact they made. My favorite hymn is "Great is Thy Faithfulness."

It has taught me to trust God more, because He's not going to change. He is my strength for today and my hope for tomorrow!

I've heard it said, "If you learn to trust God in little things, it's easier to trust Him in the big things." The more I trust Him, the more I recognize how He shows himself faithful in my life. And WOW did the big things show up! An indescribable tragedy in my family, then breast cancer and lymphoma. I knew immediately who to turn to. He gave me peace and carried me through it all! Who am I to deserve that? In Him, I am a child of the King! He is my portion, and my hope is in Him. He was faithful. He *is* faithful! His mercies are new every morning!

Lord! I'm so thankful for Your faithfulness. You promised You would never leave me or forsake me. You don't just show up, You're always there! Help me to recognize Your constant presence in my life. Truly, I need You every minute of every hour of every day! Amen.

Linda Teel
President
Singing Church Women of Oklahoma, East

Star Gazing

*The heavens declare the glory of God,
the skies proclaim the work of his hands.*
PSALM 19:1 (NIV)

I love living in the country, away from the noise and lights of the city. One of my favorite things about country living is coming home after dark on a clear night. On those nights, I can never go inside without standing in the yard, looking up and admiring the moon and all the stars that fill the vast night sky! No matter how often I do this, it never ceases to amaze me!

In that moment, I feel so small and insignificant. As I search for The Dippers, I praise God for His creation, and the words of one song always come to my mind:

> *"When I gaze into the night skies,
> And see the work of Your fingers;
> The moon and stars suspended in space.
> Oh, what is man that You are mindful of him?"*

I remember the first time I heard that song. I was attending summer youth camp at Falls Creek in Davis, Oklahoma. I was part of the choir that week, and this was one of the songs we learned. My love for singing in a choir grew significantly as we sang this song during an evening worship service, one hot July night, in an open-air tabernacle.

How amazing it is that the God who created all those stars, and holds each of them in place, cares about me—and you!

Thank you, Father, for Your amazing creation! Your creation declares Your glory. Help me to declare Your glory as I strive to live for You each day. Amen.

Deanne Maynard
Historian
Singing ChurchWomen of Oklahoma, West

Assistant
Oklahoma Baptist Children's Chorus

The Majesty and Glory of Your Name, words by Linda Lee Johnson, music by Tom Fettke, ©1979 Word Music, LLC, Wordspring Music, LLC

He Sings Over Us!

The Lord your God is with you, the Mighty Warrior who saves. He will take great delight in you; in his love he will no longer rebuke you, but will rejoice over you with singing.
ZEPHANIAH 3:17 (NIV)

God has certainly used music throughout my life to encourage me, challenge me, correct me and guide me. This has happened in so many ways and on such a regular basis that I did not even try to pick one instance to share. What did immediately come to mind was a passage of scripture that we recently sang with our Kids Choir.

God loves us. He is with us. We know this because we read it throughout Scripture. What jumps out to me in this verse is that the God who was powerful enough to create all things, the God who is mighty enough to sustain all things, the God who will judge all things, *rejoices over **me**—with singing!*

God gave us the incredible gift of music. We use it to praise Him, express our love for Him and to proclaim Him. What an awesome thing it is to know God sings over us. He delights in us. He rejoices over us so much that He sings.

I am like that, too. When I am happy, I sing. When I am grateful, I sing. When I am sad or weary ... I sing. I sing, shout and rejoice whenever I think of what God has done for me. I truly am made in the image of God.

Dear Father, I have lived in Your love and enjoyed and experienced Your grace, mercy and presence for so many years. I smile today when I think about You enjoying me so much that You sing. May the way I live my life today continue to bring You joy and give You even more reason to sing. Amen.

Randy Holt
Director
Oklahoma Student Worship Choir
Singing Churchmen of Oklahoma

Miss Martha with the Dance Moves

*Train up a child in the way he should go;
even when he is old he will not depart from it.*
PROVERBS 22:6 (ESV)

I was raised in a legalistic church that did not encourage independent Bible study or memorizing scripture. When I was an adult and was saved, God led me to a Bible teaching, Southern Baptist church where I have been a member for more than 20 years. I struggled with the need to "catch up" or the place to serve when I felt I did not have the knowledge or the skills to teach scripture or share the Gospel. I sat in many Bible study sessions and discipleship groups but continued to feel like I would never find my place in this new Church. But God had a plan for me—Vacation Bible School!

I have a music background, so I began to lead the Music rotation every year and continue to this day. I studied the songs, learned every motion and enjoyed sharing these songs with children. One young child identified me to her grandparents as "Miss Martha with the dance moves," and her family calls me that to this day.

The songs were fun and entertaining, but something began to happen to me beyond making sure all the children could sing and perform the songs. I realized one day "I've memorized scripture." Every song was straight from the Bible! Every year there was also a song that shared the plan of salvation. In addition to having fun, the children were learning to recite scripture, and the decisions we counted at the end of the week included children who had learned the ABCs (Accept, Believe, Confess). Seeds of the Gospel had been planted, and they were opening their hearts to Jesus. The music we adults sing in our worship services is meant to do the same—lead us to Scripture and salvation.

Now I teach a small group of adult women, and we work weekly to learn God's Word and hide it in our hearts. I'm also part of the Worship team each Sunday. So, never underestimate God! He will direct your path and work through you to bring Glory to His name.

Father, direct my path and make me bold to share your Word with a lost and dying world. Amen.

Martha Hoffman
Alto 2 Section Leader
Singing Churchwomen of Oklahoma, East

Sing That All May Know Jesus

In the same way, let your light shine before others, that they may see your good deeds and glorify your Father in heaven.
MATTHEW 5:16 (NIV)

When I was 16, I was discovering my singing voice. I couldn't read music, but I could pick up a song quickly and make a decent sound.

Up to this age, I was trying my hardest not to sing in choir. So when I was old enough to choose an elective class, I chose anything but choir. However, at East Bay Christian High School, I was placed in choir even though I didn't want to sing. But the truth is, I liked it.

At this same time, my Dad suffered a life-changing stroke. This was devastating to my family and me. Our main provider could no longer provide for and support us. We became his support. As you can imagine, we went through some very difficult times, and during this time, my choir teacher gave me a song to sing as a solo. It was "Thank You, Lord" by Dan Burgess.

> *"I thank You, Lord,*
> *For the trials that come my way.*
> *In that way I can grow each day*
> *As I let You lead.*
> *And I thank you, Lord,*
> *For the patience those trials bring.*
> *In the process of growing,*
> *I can learn to care."*

This song taught me how to thank God in the midst of trials. "Thank you, Lord" became my prayer as a young teenager, and as a result, my relationship with the Lord grew. For the first time, I saw that music was a way for me to share my faith and allow others to witness the Lord's work in and through my life.

As I began singing more often, my mother bought me a new songbook, and she wrote the heart of Matthew 5:16 in my book: "Sing That All May Know Jesus!" To this day, I use this phrase as my personal mission statement.

Thank you, Father, for trials that bring me closer to You. Thank you for the patience those trials bring. Thank you for loving, caring for and leading me. May You be seen and glorified in all I do. Amen.

Jeff Elkins
Minister of Worship
Tulsa, First
Singing Churchmen of Oklahoma

Thank You, Lord, Dan Burgess, ©1975 Light Publishing, Waco, Texas

Wait On the Lord

But they that wait upon the Lord shall renew their strength; they shall mount up with wings as eagles; they shall run and not be weary; and they shall walk, and not faint.
Isaiah 40:31 (KJV)

One summer, I went with a bus load of YWA's from Oklahoma to Ridgecrest, North Carolina, for YWA Week. The invitation song was "Wherever He Leads I'll Go" by B.B. McKinney. Through that song, I felt God calling me to be a missionary.

The following summer was my first missionary trip. I spent six weeks on Indian reservations in Arizona. At camp we learned a new song. It was "Teach Me, Lord, To Wait" by Stuart Hamblen. It was based on Isaiah 40:31. I had never read that verse, much less sung it.

> *"Teach me Lord to wait down on my knees,*
> *Till in Your own good time You answer my pleas.*
> *Teach me not to rely on what others do,*
> *But to wait in prayer for an answer from You."*
>
> *"They that wait upon the Lord shall renew their strength.*
> *They shall mount up with wings as eagles.*
> *They shall run and not be weary.*
> *They shall walk and not faint.*
> *Teach me, Lord, teach me, Lord, to wait."*

Those two "summer songs" have directed my life. Many times I've been asked about my goals for the next 5 years, 10 years, 20 years, etc. I always made up something, because I didn't know where God might lead me. I was waiting for God to lead me, and He always has. Through times of joy and times of difficulty, He gives me strength. He keeps His Word—His promises are true. The melody of the song I learned at Indian Camp years ago still plays in my heart and mind even though I have never heard it sung since.

Father God, You are mighty and You are faithful. Thank you for Your Word and the power it has when set to music. I praise You for melodies that speak through the years. May all that I say and all that I do be for Your glory. Amen.

Martha Peck
Alto 1 Section Leader
Singing ChurchWomen of Oklahoma, East

Teach Me, Lord, To Wait, Stuart Hamblen, ©1953, renewed 1981 Hamblen Music Co.

The Checklist

Without holiness, no one will see the Lord.
Hebrews 12:14 (NIV)

My earliest memory of a checklist is not necessarily a good one. At FBC Fort Smith, there was a lady in every kid's Sunday School class who sat at a check-in desk. You couldn't enter the class without getting past her. I've since learned that she was a sweet lady, but to my first grade buddies and me, she was intimidating with her fiery eyes and foreboding countenance! There she sat with a three-ring notebook, golf pencil and self-righteous judgment expecting to put a check mark in every box across the top of the card—boxes that represented things we were to have done the week prior or items we were to bring. The moment our eyes met, the inquisition began!

It often went something like this. Name? Check. Bible? Check. Offering? Check. Quarterly? Nope. (I'm sure it was behind my bed or under the car seat). Invite a friend? Nope (all my friends were in line behind me for cryin' out loud). Memory verse? Oh PLEASE!

Can we just get to the feltboard Bible story, the graham crackers and red Kool-Aid? I just couldn't seem to get a check mark in every box. I'm sure that sweet lady was just as relieved as I was to let me pass. Embarrassing? Yes. Important? Yes. The idea was to train us early for the more serious checklists to come.

From those early days until now, my life has been full of exposure to spiritual checklists found in the great hymns which has served to keep me focused on the most important things in life. A checklist for my life? Yes indeed!

One of my favorite "checklist hymns" is "Take Time to Be Holy" written by William Longstaff.

> *"Take time to be holy, speak oft with thy Lord;*
> *Abide in Him always, and feed on His word.*
> *Make friends of God's children, help those who are weak;*
> *Forgetting in nothing, His blessing to seek."*

The first grade Sunday School checklist pales in comparison to the one that confronts us in this hymn! The words penned in this text provide the Christ-follower a clear path of commitment to the Lord and service to others. As we continue to sing the truths and challenges found in our hymns, let's allow the words provide a checklist for our devotion to Christ and service to His Kingdom.

Dear Lord, may I always take time to be with You, speak with You, and abide in You. Amen.

James Bradford
Minister of Music
OKC, Quail Springs
Orchestra Director
Singing Churchmen of Oklahoma

Bigger Pants is Not an Option

Dear brothers and sisters, when troubles of any kind come your way, consider it an opportunity for great joy.
JAMES 1:2 (NLT)

I can't tell you how many time during my 50-plus years of ministry I've thought: "God, can't I just have a few days of peace. I really want to live for You, but it seems that the more I try to put You first, the more I get beaten up by the world. And the more I realize how far I fall short of what You have in store for me."

If you have also had that thought, then congratulations, God is at work in your life! When your pants are too tight, you can either diet or be uncomfortable! When God stresses your life, He wants you to become more like Jesus. You can say either "Yes" or "No." "Yes" enables God's power in your life. "No" usually brings more distress and disease.

As a child of God, getting "bigger pants" is not an option—a

Christian can never be comfortable out of God's will. The only option is to become more like Jesus by giving Him complete control over everything.

> "My Savior is the Lord and King.
> He has control of everything.
> He loves me, and He bids me sing.
> He gives His song to me."

Our strength is completely inadequate to deal with the challenges we face. This truth plays out in every aspect of our existence. When God gives us the realization that we can't save ourselves, we are finally open to ask Jesus to be our Savior. When our strength is gone and all that's left is God, He is ready to prove that He's all we need.

Father, help me to see You at work in my life and ministry, especially when I am discouraged and feel like giving up. Amen.

Walter Grady
Minister of Music, Retired
Singing Churchmen of Oklahoma

Jesus is the Song, David Danner, ©1979 Broadman Press (SESAC), (admin. by LifeWay Worship)

Why Do I Sing?

My heart is confident in you, O God; no wonder I can sing your praises with all my heart! Wake up, lyre and harp! I will wake the dawn with my song. I will thank you, LORD, among all the people. I will sing your praises among the nations.
PSALMS 108:1-3 (NLT)

King David's confidence was in the Lord. God clearly confirmed to David that He was with him in his struggles and despair. David often sang himself into assurance in the Lord with great joy! He could not help but sing, and he most likely did not sing at the pianissimo level, instead at fortissimo! To "wake the dawn" would certainly have taken a powerful song!

Why do I sing praises to the Lord? Like David, I have dealt with my own struggles and despair. At one time in my life I was at my lowest place. My husband was an infantry officer deployed into fierce combat; I was plunged into deep despair and my joy had been replaced by worry and fear. An old hymn being sung in a Sunday evening worship service leaped into my heart and the words filled my soul!

> *"Great is Thy faithfulness!*
> *Great is Thy faithfulness!*
> *Morning by morning new mercies I see.*
> *All I have needed Thy hand hath provided!"*

The words captured my attention. I realized that God was all I needed to give me real peace. That song of assurance lifted me and filled my heart with joy, and it still resounds to this day regardless of circumstances!

Singing to the Lord is not merely an option. Psalm 100 commands us to *"make a joyful noise unto the Lord!"* In fact, the Bible gives 50 commands to sing!

How robust is your song of confidence and thanks to the Lord? Sing your song with joy. Sing it with passion. Sing it strong! What a magnificent way to please Him!

Dear God, thank You for being our almighty rock, our confidence, our song. May I continually have a song of praise in my heart! I sing with great joy and thanksgiving knowing You are my Savior and Deliverer! Amen.

Betty Brown
Secretary
Singing Church Women of Oklahoma, West

The Lord is Near

*The Lord is near to all who call upon Him,
to all who call upon Him in truth.*
PSALM 145:18 (NASB)

I was on a social media platform a couple of months ago when I was tagged by a young woman who said that I had been her pastor in the 70s. She said that she would never forget me singing "My Lord is Near Me All the Time" at church. I had not thought of the song in years. Yet her mentioning it brought back a flood of memories. Some of those memories were like storm clouds, dark and foreboding. Others were sweet and tender like a gentle rain.

> "I've seen it in the lightning, heard it in the thunder,
> And felt it in the rain;
> My Lord is near me all the time,
> My Lord is near me all the time."

The one thing that is certain, is that though there have been stormy times and calm, tearful times and times of joy, the Lord has walked with me through them all. He is ever present and gives compassionate strength to me, every day of my life.

In recent days, both my wife and I have had more than our share of health issues. We are in the later years of our lives. But we rest in the arms of our Lord, knowing that He is always there to give us calm assurance of His presence as we walk life's journey together.

The writer of Hebrews said, *"for He Himself has said, 'I will never desert you, nor will I ever forsake you'* (Hebrews 13:5b). Jesus said, *"… I am with you always, even to the end of the age"* (Matthew 28:20b). The assurance of His presence gives a comfort beyond measure.

Precious Lord, I thank you that You walk the paths of life with me. Help me to always be aware of Your presence and direction in my life. Amen.

BJ Hall
Minister of Music
Tulsa, Easton Heights
Singing Churchmen of Oklahoma

My Lord Is Near Me All the Time, Barbara Fowler Gaultney, ©1960 by Broadman Press (SESAC)

Quiet Answers

Your strength will lie in quiet confidence.
ISAIAH 30:15 (CSB)

Listening to Christian radio in the car, I was driving to a job interview feeling severely underqualified and wondering why I had even applied. After all, I had just failed a typing test during an interview with a different employer because my fingers were misaligned on the keyboard. I knew it would be a hurdle—possibly a veritable mountain—for this company to choose me as their next employee. Praying with my eyes open (of course), I felt a peace wash over me from the very first notes of Kelly Nelon (Thompson) Clark's song "Quiet Answers."

"*I sometimes ask for miracles when I kneel to pray and then expect the mountain to be taken from my way .... God sends a quiet answer to my prayer ... just as great as miracles that come in mighty ways .... You don't have to move the earth to let me know that You're still there. Just send a quiet answer to my prayer.*"

I was praying for God to move a mountain, hoping for a miracle, but what I really needed to pray for was the faith to let Him do what He does best. The peace God provided allowed me to exhibit confidence like no candidate my future boss had ever seen, and that was what impressed him most. The next ten years of my career began that day, allowing me to be an integral part of a Christian company and grow in ways I never imagined.

The children of Israel found it difficult to wait quietly. Isaiah declared they weren't even willing! The disciples fell short of faith in Matthew 17:20. We all fall short. The next time you need a mountain moved, ask God to enlarge your faith and look for quiet answers.

Father, thank You for the reminders in music and Scripture of what You can do when my life is filled with mountains to overcome. Give me the faith to let You move them in Your own way and the confident assurance of Your presence within me. Help me be grateful for the quiet answers You send. Amen.

Patricia Farewell
Secretary
Singing ChurchWomen of Oklahoma, West
Former Coordinator
SCW/SCM/OBS

Quiet Answers, Don Koch, ©1990 Benson Music

Step by Step for Bible Study

*In all your ways acknowledge him,
and he will make your paths straight.*
Proverbs 3:6 (NIV)

I'm an avid journaler. Every morning I journal about the happenings of the previous day, things to come that day and what's in the future. Sometimes I include my devotional or Bible study notes. Sometimes I ramble on about nothing in particular. Often I express my emotions in writing.

In the front of each journal, I affix a label with the lines to a very simple song that Rich Mullins sings:

"Oh God, You are my God; and I will ever praise You. I will seek You in the morning and I will learn to walk in Your ways; and step by step You'll lead me and I will follow You all of my days."

What a sweet and simple message that is.

As I sit at my desk, I begin each time with God by singing these words. For me, it's a meaningful way to focus on the purpose of my time with God and to discover what the Holy Spirit has to say to me. Afterward, I'm prepared to apply and commit to what God has revealed to me through His Word.

In interviews with composer Beaker Strasser, he's often asked questions about this relatively short worship song. His answer generally relates to the teaching aspect of the song. First, we recognize God as Lord. Second, we commit to praise Him. Third, this commitment leads you to seek Him as we begin each day. Fourth, our seeking prompts us to learn more about God. Fifth, this newly acquired knowledge directs as we walk in His will.

How do you approach your devotional or Bible study time? Do you intentionally seek what God has to say to you or do you just go through the motions with other things on your mind? Learn this little song. Use it as a guide for your devotional life. Allow it to expand and energize your relationship with God.

Heavenly Father, I pray that as worship leaders, we are always in step with You during our times of Bible study. Teach us how to dig into this time with a plan that allows us to experience You in a way that encourages us, teaches us and motivates us to follow You always. Amen.

Allen Kimberlin
Worship Pastor
OKC, Village
Singing Churchmen of Oklahoma

Step by Step, David (Beaker) Strasser/Michael W. Smith, ©1991 BMG Songs, Inc./Kid Brothers of St. Frank Music Publishing (ASCAP), (admin. By Brentwood-Benson Music Publishing, Inc.)

Breaking the Language Barrier

This is how God showed his love among us: he sent his one and only Son into the world that we might live through him. This is love: not that we loved God, but that he loved us and sent his Son as an atoning sacrifice for our sins. Dear friends, since God so loved us, we also ought to love one another.
JOHN 4:9-11 (NIV)

In the late 1940s, my church had an influx of war brides following World War II. Many of our soldiers had fallen in love and brought their brides back to a land of new opportunities. However, there was one major problem: the language barrier.

Back then, Oklahoma City wasn't the cultural melting pot that it is now. The ladies in the church knew something had to be done about this barrier. Especially since there was a Story these new arrivals needed to hear.

My great grandmother, a member of the church, took it upon

herself to learn a language that was just as foreign to her as her language was to these foreign women. She taught herself one simple song she could sing to reach one Japanese lady. She sang: "*Jesus loves me this I know, for the Bible tells me so.*"

Through her efforts, that Japanese lady was saved to New Life in Christ. Now, with a new song in her heart, she started a Bible class and taught her Japanese friends a song about the Savior she had fallen in love with. Using the language of her faraway homeland, she taught them to sing: "*What a friend we have in Jesus, all our sins and griefs to bear. What a privilege to carry, everything to God in prayer.*"

Father in Heaven, thank you that Your love knows no barriers; that Your grace knows no bounds. Empower me, by Your Spirit, to break through barriers to reach those who desperately need to know the Savior. Amen.

Brandon Chenoweth
Singing Churchmen of Oklahoma

Sheltering Arms, Comforting Arms

He will tend his flock like a shepherd. he gathers the lambs in his arms and carries them close to his heart.
ISAIAH 40:1 (NIV)

My mother was dying. She entered the hospital for an outpatient procedure, but the doctors surprisingly found a problem for which there was no solution. She never returned home.

Mom walked into the hospital on her own power, yet in one week, she could not walk unassisted. In two weeks, she could not stand. In three weeks, she could not sit up. And, at four weeks, she was gone. As progressive debilitation overtook her body, my constant prayer was for God to wrap His arms around Mom and to take her gently, without pain or suffering.

When saying my prayers on the morning of what was to be the day she died, I repeated my request for God to hold Mom in His arms. Suddenly, that little voice in my head replied, "She has always been in My arms." Immediately, I gained peace and consolation, knowing that Mom was safe. God loves and cares for all His children … all the time.

The words of the song "Sheltered in the Arms of God" came to mind and replayed in my heart all day.

> *"Soon I shall feel the call from Heaven's portals.*
> *Come home, my child, it's the last mile you must trod.*
> *I'll fall asleep and wake in God's new heaven,*
> *For I'm sheltered in the arms of God."*

I gained comfort by knowing that Mom was lovingly wrapped in the sheltering arms of God as she departed this life. The assurance of God's abundant love, regardless of the circumstances or situation, is powerful. God is always in control.

Dear Lord, while it is painful to lose loved ones, we are assured by the knowledge that they are rejoicing with You in Glory. Thank you for the gift of comfort during our times of grief. Amen.

Barbara Williams
Immediate Past President
Singing ChurchWomen of Oklahoma, East

Sheltered in the Arms of God, Dottie Rambo/Jimmie Davis, ©1969 Peermusic, Ltd.

When Melody Turns Into Movement

Surely goodness and mercy shall follow me all the days of my life, and I shall dwell in the house of the Lord forever.
Psalm 23:6 (ESV)

In 1998, I had my first opportunity to attend a leadership camp called Super Summer. The camp was hosted at Oklahoma Baptist University. I was in the seventh grade and couldn't wait to have another new experience in my faith. That week was unforgettable. It took my heart and faith on a journey that set a new course and mission I would follow the rest of my life. The worship leader that week was Billy Foote. One of his songs that he led us in was titled "Goodness and Mercy."

For the first time in my life, I started to understand that the lyrical content I was singing had a much deeper meaning than a band on stage or a cool melody. We were singing scripture! This scripture was alive and challenging us, and the melody was requesting our hearts to move into a new understanding of what it means to follow God.

As I meditated on the lyrics of the song, I knew the Lord was inviting me into a calling. I was going to surrender my life to ministry and serve Him for the rest of my days. I am so grateful that Billy chose to write songs based on the Word of God.

May we as the Church never lose sight of why we worship. May we always come with an expectant heart that God is going to do something amazing in our lives, regardless of our preferred expression or style of song. May we let melodies turn into movements. Amen.

Cody Dunbar
Worship Pastor
Yukon, Trinity
Singing Churchmen of Oklahoma

Goodness and Mercy, Billy Forte, ©1993 Centricity Music Publishing

The Vastness of His Love

> *And I pray that you and all God's holy people will have the power to understand the greatness of Christ's love. I pray that you can understand how wide and how long and how high and how deep that love is.*
> EPHESIANS 3:18 (ICB)

It was a quiet afternoon, when while in a reflective mood, that I came across the words to the hymn "Here Is Love" in a book I was reading.

> "Here is love, vast as the ocean,
> Loving-kindness as the flood,
> When the Prince of Life, our Ransom,
> Shed for us His precious blood.
> Who His love will not remember?
> Who can cease to sing His praise?
> He can never be forgotten,
> Throughout heav'n's eternal days."

Originally penned in Welsh by William Rees and put to music by Robert Lowery in 1876, it would go on to play a prominent role in the Welsh revival of 1904-1905.

As I read these words, I was overwhelmed by the thought of how much the Father loves me. His everlasting compassion, His unending grace, the undeserved forgiveness and mercy He has shown to me … may it never cease to amaze me. I never want to forget how much grace and love it took for me to become His child.

Father, thank You for Your gift of love to me. Thank You for reminding me of Your grace and Your mercy toward me. Let me show this love toward all those whose lives I touch today. Amen.

Barbara Billingsley
Prayer Ministry Leader
Singing ChurchWomen of Oklahoma

Desperately Valuable

You have encircled me; you have placed your hand on me.
PSALM 139:5 (CSB)

"But those are my favorite jeans," I cried to my wife. "No, Gary, I'm not fixing them anymore; they're trash." With those cryptic words, my beloved britches were discarded - like last Tuesday's trash. Alas, I was desperate to save my cherished corduroys, but it was useless. I have been in difficult situations before; however, truth be told, I've been in much more desperate times than the loss of my trousers.

Lauren Daigle's song "Hold On To Me" has a phrase: *"When I start to break in desperation underneath the weight of expectations, hold on to me."*

When was the last time you felt desperate? Desperate with confusion because of a change in a career or ministry—desperate with agony over family situations—desperate with worry over financial struggles. We all face desperate times. We long for the Lord to wrap His arms around us and hold us, whispering in our ear, "It's OK, I've got you. You are still valuable to me."

The psalmist in Psalm 139:5 wrote: *"You have encircled me; you have placed your hand on me."* The word "encircled" is a military term. It is the act of a military troop surrounding and guarding something very valuable. We need to remember that the Creator of the universe holds the world together and also holds us in His arms. He embraces us because He created us. We are His most valuable possession.

For me, I have learned I can hold my head up and walk with confidence, because I'm desperately valuable to the Lord. In the midst of difficult situations, I cannot escape His love nor can I hide from His presence.

Thank you, Lord, for Your constant care and direction in my life. Thank you for holding me in times of desperation and uncertainty. Amen.

Gary D. Canfield
Music/College Minister
Singing Churchmen of Oklahoma

Hold On To Me, Lauren Daigle/Paul Duncan/Paul Mabury, 2021 Centricity Music Publishing (ASCAP)

Hymn of God's Glory

*Who is the King of glory? The Lord of Heavens Armies—
He is the King of Glory.*
PSALM 24:10 (NLT)

As a girl growing up in the 50s and 60s, I was raised in a musical home. My father often sang and played the guitar. My mom couldn't carry a tune at all. However, she would always attempt to sing, even when criticized about singing off key.

I remember two songs she dearly loved to sing. One she sang every morning when I complained about the weather or a situation I had to face: "This is the Day That the Lord Has Made." But her very favorite was "To God Be the Glory." She always requested that song when she had the opportunity. I often begged her, "Mom, please pick a different song." She would reply, "Oh, no, that song says ***everything*** about who our God is, and we are to give Him all the glory for ***everything*** that He has done." She always emphasized the word "everything." She even had that hymn sung by the choir at her funeral. It was beautiful.

Years later, when I visited the Grand Canyon, as I stood in awe of its beauty, the song "To God Be the Glory" flooded my mind. I turned to my husband and said, "My mom would have loved this view, seeing the absolute beauty in God's creation. She would have broken into song, and I can almost hear her singing off-key:"

> "Praise the Lord, praise the Lord,
> Let the earth hear His voice;
> Praise the Lord, praise the Lord,
> Let the people rejoice;
> Oh, come to the Father, through Jesus the Son,
> And give Him the glory; great things He hath done."

As an adult, every time I hear that song, I think of how blessed I am that I had a mother who loved singing praises to our Father and giving Him the glory for *everything* He has done.

Thank you, Lord, for the beauty of this earth and for everything you have given to me. Thank you for the great things You have done in my life. Praise the Lord! Amen.

Kathy Kitterman
State Coordinator
Singing Church Women of Oklahoma

Day by Day

The Lord is my rock and my fortress and my deliverer, my God, my rock, in whom I take refuge, my shield, and the horn of my salvation, my stronghold.
Psalm 18:2 (ESV)

Comparable to Horatio Spafford writing "It is Well with My Soul" following the tragic death of his four daughters aboard the S.S. Ville du Havre on a transatlantic voyage, Swedish hymn writer Lina Sandell wrote "Day by Day" in 1865, after witnessing the drowning death of her father.

The first time I played "Day by Day," I was in high school. *"Help me then in every tribulation so to trust Thy promises, O Lord"* encouraged that young believer as I learned God's promises are true and trustworthy.

The hymn provided strength in my early 40s as I handled my cancer diagnosis. *"He whose heart is kind beyond all measure gives unto each day what He deems best"* assured me that God knew the entire, finished portrait of my life, and I was in the Master's hand.

Today, I lean on Lina's words as they teach me the deepest confidence and rest.

> *"Every day the Lord Himself is near me*
> *With a special mercy for each hour;*
> *All my cares He fain would bear, and cheer me,*
> *He whose name is Counselor and Power.*
> *The protection of His child and treasure*
> *Is a charge that on Himself He laid;*
> *'As thy days, thy strength shall be in measure,'*
> *This the pledge to me He made."*

As I face the future, the closing words of the hymn bring me abiding comfort: *"Help me, Lord, when toil and trouble meeting, Ever to take, as from a father's hand, One by one, the days, the moments fleeting, Till I reach the promised land."*

Thank you, Father, that I can trust that Your strength, Word and care for me will always be greater than the needs of my day. I lean on You to bear my burdens and direct my paths. Amen.

Laura Gandy
Worship and Evangelism Ministry Assistant
Oklahoma Baptists

From Generation to Generation

*One generation shall commend your works to another,
and shall declare your mighty acts.*
Psalm 145:4 (ESV)

Most of us have heard of the phrase "actions speak louder than words." When I was very young, after my parents had graduated from Oklahoma Baptist University, we moved to Fort Worth, Texas, where my dad attended seminary as he prepared for the pastoral ministry. When my father wasn't preaching somewhere, we attended Gambrel Street Baptist Church—a church close to the seminary. I was very small, and the church seemed huge to me. I still remember the tall ceiling, the choir and the beautiful sound of the people singing together.

One Sunday, as I stood with my parents during the congregational singing, the man singing beside me glanced my way and noticed I wasn't singing because I didn't know the words. Without speaking, he gently lowered his hymnal to share it with me. Then, with his other hand, he used a finger to follow the words line by line and stanza by stanza in the hymnal. As he pointed the way, he continued to sing and worship.

That was decades ago, and I'm sure that gentleman has passed from this earth into heaven. However, I can still vividly remember how he *showed* me the Gospel that day. It was a simple act, but one that had a profound and lasting impact on my life. Would I have eventually figured out how to read a hymn in a hymnal? Surely, I would. That man certainly didn't know I would spend my life in music ministry. Yet, the kindness of a worshipper—who cared enough to lean over to a young boy and show the kindness of God—continues to live on in my life. In my own way, I seek to do the same thing with others that I stand beside. I seek to show them The Way … and worship along the way.

God, thank you for letting us worship You as the body of Christ. Thank you for those that have spoken into my life—both by word and deed. Help me be one that passes the Gospel to someone today. Amen.

Dr. Randy C. Lind
Oklahoma Baptists
Worship & Music Ministry Partner

Made in the USA
Coppell, TX
21 April 2023